Greta Thunberg
How Dare You!

Narrated By Famed Author
Acie Cargill

Copyright © 2019 by Acie Cargill.

All rights reserved.

Published by Acie Cargill

aciecargill@gmail.com

http://aciecargill.com

ISBN: 9781696422666

Imprint: Independently published

Formatted - Brenda Van Niekerk

brenda@triomarketers.com

Website Design - Brenda Van Niekerk

http://triomarketers.com

Synopsis

Climate activist Greta Thunberg has had a very busy and important month since she arrived in New York by sailboat from England. She has participated in 4 climate strikes. Two in New York, one in Washington DC in front of the White House, and one in Montreal in Canada. She also spoke in two very important places, the US Congress and the United Nations General Assembly. She has also been interviewed several times for television, radio, and newspapers. She is in demand. Greta has become a very important person here in America.

This 10,000 word booklet describes her appearances and also describes what climate change means and how it is going to affect everyone. One important part of the booklet is a transcription of her speech to the UN General Assembly for their Climate Summit on Sept 23, 2019. It was an emotional speech. Usually her speeches are not very emotional, but in this one she was angry and sad and trying to shame the global leaders for their climate inactivity. "How dare you!" She really doesn't like when leaders claim to be sympathetic to the cause of the young people, but then do nothing to help. She wants them to walk their talk.

President Trump sarcastically called her a very happy young girl with a bright and wonderful future ahead of her. This was after her scathing speech at the UN. She answered Trump on Twitter by changing her profile to say she is a happy, young girl with a bright and wonderful future ahead of her.

About the Author

Acie Cargill is a poet, a songwriter, and a prose writer. He studied poetry with USA Poet Laureate Mark Strand and Illinois Poet Laureate Gwendolyn Brooks. He studied novel writing with Thomas Berger, who wrote Little Big Man (that Arthur Penn made into a movie with Dustin Hoffman in the lead role). Cargill also studied journalism with instructor Jean Daily. His work is a synthesis of all these styles.

He is a member of American Mensa and formerly Edited the Mensa Journal of Poetry. He also is a member of the Grammy Association, and The US Quill and Scroll Society.

Cargill is a vegetarian, a former holistic physician, a musical performer on a variety of instruments, an environmental activist, a lecturer, medical reviewer, a lover, and a seer.

Website

http://aciecargill.com

Contact

aciecargill@gmail.com

Other Books Written by the Author:

Puerto Rico

Aberrations

Chronicles

Terrorism

Modern Love

Ends and odds

Illiana: The Border Area Between Illinois and Indiana

Pullman

Che and Fidel - A Reading Play of the Cuban Revolution

Celia Sanchez - A Play of the Cuban Revolution

Paschke - A Play

Gwendolyn Brooks: A Play

Rasputin - A Play

Nietzsche - A Play

Bob Dylan, The Early Years - A Musical Play

Michael Jackson - A Play

Einstein - A Biographical Play

El Chapo - A Play In 3 Acts

Raisins and Roaches - A Three Month Diary of a Crack Addict

Susan B. Anthony - A Biographical Play

Kankakee

Harriet Tubman - A Biographical Play

Tesla - A Biographical Play

Vegan Saint - A Play in 3 Acts

Martin Luther King, Jr - A Play

Great Migration: A Play in 3 Acts

George Pullman - A Play in Three Acts

Frederick Douglass - A Biographical Play

Freud - A Biographical Play in 3 Acts

The Underground Railroad - An Educational Play

Payton, Jordan, Ali - A Biographical Play

Mr. Nobody - A Play

The Kid From Left Field - A Play

Puerto Rico, A Dream of Independence - A Play in 3 Acts

Crack Madness - A Monologue Play

Johnny Appleseed - A Family Play

Dr. Jekll and Mr. Hyde - A Modernized Play

Obama - Obama - A Play In 3 Acts

Will Rogers - A Biographical Monologue

Merle Haggard - A Biographical Monologue

Mother Teresa - A Biographical Monologue

Gwendolyn Brooks - A Biographical Monologue

Love Life of Susan B. Anthony - A Monologue Play

Sojourner Truth - A Biographical Monologue plus Narrator

Harriet Tubman and The Underground Railroad - A Play

Helen Keller, Words and Wisdom - A Biographical Play

Eugene Debs and the 1894 Pullman Strike - A Play

The Rising - A Play

Walt Disney - A Biographical One Act Play

The Experiments of Dr. Victor Frankenstein - A Play - Based on the novel by Mary Shelley

Karl Marx - A One Act Play

Martin Luther at The Diet of Worms - A One Act Play

Martin Luther King: Monologue and Narrator Play

Frederick Douglass - Monologue and Narrator Play

Kaepernick - A One Act Play

Settling South Holland - A Play In 2 Acts

Kaepernick - A Full-Length Play

My Son Died From An Overdose - A Play

Overdose - A One Act Play

Always a Marine First

Erotic Muslim Polygamy

George Dolton's Bridge to Freedom Underground Railroad - A One-Act Play

Greta Thunberg - A One-Act Play About Climate Change

A Brief History of the Philippines

Goat With No Horns - Voodoo Cannibals in Haiti

Johnny Cash - Monologue Play

Muhammad Words Of Wisdom

Jesus Words Of Wisdom

Bob Hope - Biographical Monologue

The Cargills of Graves County, Ky

Keith Raniere and the NXIVM Sex Club

Words of Wisdom – Native Americans, Ancient Greeks, Buddha and African-Americans

Words of Wisdom – Mark Twain, Benjamin Franklin, Shakespeare and Solomon

The Trial of Eddie Gallagher, Navy SEAL

Climate Crisis - A Plan to Prevent Future Flooding

Yukio Mishima - Life, Death, Hara Kiri

My "Cuzin Willie" Nelson - A Biographical Monologue

The World's Most Amazing Person, Elon Musk

The Beatles: Early Years - A One-Act Play

Red Summer Race Riot Chicago 1919 - Eyewitnesses John Harris and Ida B. Wells

Jeffrey Epstein - Illicit Kicks and Retribution

Gandhi - A Brief Biography

Jeffrey Epstein - Death Controversy

Greta Thunberg - Coming to America

Jeffrey Epstein Honeypots - Wealth, Women, and Girls

Tom Dreesen - Monologue Play

Roswell 1947

Table of Contents

1. Introduction

Not since the civil war has there been an issue that seems to so severely divide American opinion. Then it was slavery and now it is climate change. Not just in America. The entire free world is divided. Climate change activists and climate change deniers. And the people on both sides are emotional and vehement. Anger. Even hatred.

There is a correlation with climate change denial and political conservatism. They like more jobs. Higher pay. Even at the cost of environmental destruction. The people in this group don't really believe that the environment is being destroyed by our excess consumption and emissions. They think it is just natural cycles and many think everything is God's will. And they believe it intensely.

Burn those fossil carbon sources with no limits and no restrictions. For heat and electricity and especially automotive transportation needs and now air flight usage after Greta Thunberg brought the carbon footprint of flying to the forefront with her 2-week ocean voyage from England to the US.

Reducing the costs is everything to the conservatives. Get more natural gas through fracking even though the process negatively affects the drinking water and farm water of large areas. Drill more oil wells in pristine wilderness areas and in the oceans where some gets spilled every year. Build more risky pipelines to transport it. Risky for spills and risky for explosions. Expand the coal mining areas. More jobs, but more desecration of the environment.

The main spokesperson for the climate change deniers is the President of the United States, Donald Trump. There are others of course. All over the world. He seems to be the most visible and outspoken. He really believes there is no climate change caused by human planetary abuse. Of course, he is also a consummate politician who likes his office and wants to appease his voters with relaxed environmental restrictions and more jobs that are somewhat dependent on more pollution.

He has many enemies. People who are shocked and offended by his abolishing many of the environmental progresses made over the years. Dump mining wastes in the rivers. Open wilderness areas for mining and drilling. Loosening many of the environmental safeguards because they are not good for business. It seems that he just doesn't care about environmental regression. He only cares about the money that can be saved, and profits increased. More jobs. Better pay. More votes.

His most visible opponent is Greta Thunberg, a sixteen year old originally from Sweden. There have always been defenders of wildlife and the environment, but they have not been so loud as they are now. Greta is quiet, but her followers are loud and boisterous and numerous. Sometimes the climate strikes that she initiates can mobilize a couple of million people all over the Earth. Most are young. Most are teenagers. Some even younger. Greta has made them aware that they are in danger of not having much of a future.

It is the young versus the old. The old want to keep enjoying life like they are doing now, and the young want changes made. And they want action now. Not eventually. They want laws enacted that may stem some of the environmental destruction of this planet. The young want changes. This is their world. They are the future and they want the destruction stopped. Now.

2. What is climate change?

What does all this mean? What is all this fuss about? If there is global warming, a lot of people in the North think that means their winters will not be so severe. But it doesn't always work that way. There are other factors and their winters might be colder even with the global warming. Weather is not always predictable. The Earth has been sort of stabilized in its weather patterns for a long time with very little changes in the global temperature as a whole.

Everybody ha experienced colder winters and hotter summers and everything in between. There is always a variety of weather. The variations that we notice are probably not really important in determining change. There have always been variety from year to year or even decade to decade or century to century or millennium to millennium. We adjust to it and hopefully we can survive.

Humans seem to be an adaptable species and have been able to establish a lifestyle everywhere on this planet. Any climate. Maybe any climate change. Maybe. But if the climate changes, the nature changes. People who live close to nature may have more difficulty adapting to the changes. If they do, then they survive. If they don't. then they die off. Just like many of the animals who disappear. And the plants. Species. Gone. Extinction.

The climate system receives nearly all of its energy from the sun, with a relatively tiny amount from earth's interior. The climate system also gives off energy to outer space. The energy moving through Earth's climate system finds expression in weather. Long-term averages of weather in a region constitute the region's climate. Climate change is a long-term, sustained trend of change in climate. Human activities can also change the climate, and are presently driving climate change through global warming. This describes the average effect on a global scale. Climate change also describes how different geographical regions are affected differently.

Greenhouse gases, such as carbon dioxide from emissions of burning fossil fuels and also discharges from volcanoes, methane and nitrous oxide heat the climate system by trapping infrared light from the sun. We like some of that because life is based on having warmth absorbed by the earth, the oceans, and all living beings. The scientific consensus on climate change is "that the climate is changing and that these changes are in large part caused by human activities and it is largely irreversible, at least by our current level of technology. The climate protestors are hoping our scientists will develop a way to cleanse some of those greenhouse gases from the atmosphere.

The potential future effects of global climate change include more frequent wildfires, longer periods of drought in some regions and an increase in the number, duration and intensity of tropical storms. Global climate change has already had observable effects on the environment. Glaciers have shrunk, ice on rivers and lakes is breaking up earlier, plant and animal ranges have shifted and trees are flowering sooner.

Effects that scientists had predicted in the past would result from global climate change are now occurring, such as loss of sea ice, accelerated sea level rise and longer, more intense heat waves. The net damage costs of climate change are likely to be significant and to increase over time

Scientists have high confidence that global temperatures will continue to rise for decades to come, largely due to greenhouse gases produced by human activities. The Intergovernmental Panel on Climate Change (IPCC), which includes more than 1,300 scientists from the United States and other countries, forecasts a temperature rise of 2.5 to 10 degrees Fahrenheit over the next century.

So, the Earth's average temperature has increased about 2 degrees Fahrenheit during the 20th century. What's the big deal? Two degrees may sound like a small amount, but it's an unusual event in our planet's recent history. Earth's climate record, preserved in tree rings, ice cores, and coral reefs, shows that the global average temperature is stable over long periods of time. Furthermore, small changes in temperature correspond to enormous changes in the environment.

For example, at the end of the last ice age, when the Northeast United States was covered by more than 3,000 feet of ice, average temperatures were only 5 to 9 degrees cooler than today.

3. How will the Earth be affected by the climate change?

Yes, climate change is going to affect almost everyone sooner or later. Global climate is projected to continue to change over this century and beyond. The magnitude of climate change beyond the next few decades depends primarily on the amount of heat-trapping gases emitted globally, and how sensitive the Earth's climate is to those emissions. The temperature rise will not be, uniform or smooth across the country or over time.

The length of the growing season) has been increasing nationally since the 1980s, with the largest increases occurring in the western United States, affecting ecosystems and agriculture. Across the United States, the growing season is projected to continue to lengthen. The increases will be considerably smaller if heat-trapping gas emissions are reduced.

Average U.S. precipitation has increased since 1900, but some areas have had Even larger increases and some areas have had decreases. More winter and spring precipitation is projected for the northern United States, and less for the Southwest. Projections suggest that the recent trend towards increased heavy precipitation events will continue.

Droughts in the Southwest and heat waves periods of abnormally hot weather lasting days to weeks everywhere are projected to become more intense, and cold waves less intense everywhere. Summer temperatures are projected to continue rising and extreme heat days are projected to occur every two or three years over most of the nation.

The intensity, frequency and duration of North Atlantic hurricanes, as well as the frequency of the strongest (Category 4 and 5) hurricanes, have all increased since the early 1980s. The relative contributions of human and natural causes to these increases are still uncertain. Global sea level has risen by about 8 inches since reliable record keeping began in 1880. It is projected to rise another 1 to 4 feet by 2100 AD. This is the result of added water from melting land ice and the expansion of seawater as it warms.

In the next several decades, storm surges and high tides could combine with sea level rise and land subsidence to further increase flooding in many regions. Sea level rise will continue past 2100 because the oceans take a very long time to respond to warmer conditions at the Earth's surface. The Arctic Ocean is expected to become essentially ice free in summer before 2050 AD.

Here are some probable regional effects.

Northeast. Heat waves, heavy downpours and sea level rise

Northwest. Sea level rise, erosion, inundation, increasing wildfires, insect outbreaks Southeast. Sea level rise. extreme heat. decreased water availability Midwest. Extreme heat, heavy downpours, flooding, risks to the Great Lakes.

Southwest. Increased heat, drought and insect outbreaks, wildfires, erosion

4. Greta at the Climate Strikes

She gave this short statement in Montreal at the climate strike on why she has drawn the ire of right-wing politicians like Trump and Bernier. "I don't understand why grownups would choose to mock teenagers talking about the science instead of doing something good. Their world view is threatened by us. We are having so much impact that they want to silence us."

She is very popular with the young people of Canada and hundreds of thousands of them came out to march for the strike. As usual, Greta stayed mostly in the background. It was not a fiery speech that people came out for. They just wanted her to be present even if she was in a different city than most of them. She was in Montreal and the young people were marching in cities coast to coast in Canada.

One of the highlights of her Montreal visit was time to sit with the premier of Canada, Trudeau. They had a very polite conversation. Trudeau is running for re-election right now and was the only candidate who came to meet Greta and support her marching against climate change. He says he is a believer in her cause and is promoting legislation to reduce carbon dioxide emissions. He is a young man himself and wants to live in a world without climate change himself.

The previous week, Greta was in New York taking part in her largest climate strike to date. It is estimated that 4 million people were in the streets around the world protesting the lack of action against climate change. New York alone might have had ½ million protesters, certainly enough to attract political attention from the adult world. Well, there was not much. Not even a slight mention from the President or any of the Republicans in Washington. Almost like they were under orders. Rehearsed in their silence. Shouldn't they have been at least interested in climate change and preserving the world for the future. But no. Nothing. And none of the Democratic hopefuls either. Were they just being polite to the young demonstrators to avoid stealing their thunder?

The week before that Greta was at a strike in front of the White House. Thousands of marchers but non sig of recognition from the man and his family who live in the White House. Not an invitation for Greta to speak to the President for a short time. Just to be polite. But no. It didn't happen. It had been quite a month for Greta since arriving in New York after a two week sailboat voyage from England to avoid the carbon footprint of the plane ride.

A couple of days later she was invited to speak to the US Congress. She decided to just pass out a handout detailing the scientific evidence and possibilities associated with climate change. She was having quite a week. Of course, the biggest moment of the month was on September 23 when she got to speak to the General Assembly of the United Nations. That invitation was the reason she was here in the US.

Here is a rough transcription of her speech that day. An emotional speech that was unusual for her. Usually she is basically stoic, but this time there were some tears and some anger. At the end is the facetious tweet made by President Trump about her and her reply back to him as she revised her profile.

5. Greta at the United Nations General Assembly in New York

UN Narrator: Greta. Your first climate strike was a lonely event just a little over a year ago. And in the intervening time you have sparked the interest of millions of children around the globe. Demanding action for climate change. What is your message for world leaders today?

Greta: My message is that we will be watching you. This is all wrong. I shouldn't be up here. I should be back at school on the other side of the ocean.

Yes. You come to us young people for hope. How dare you! You have stolen my dreams and my childhood with your empty words. And yet I am one of the lucky ones. People ae suffering. People are dying. Our ecosystems are collapsing. We are in the beginning of a mass extinction and all you can talk about is the money and fairy tales of eternal economic growth. How dare you!

For more than thirty years the science has been crystal clear. How dare you to keep looking away and come here saying that you are doing enough. And the politics and solutions needed are still nowhere in sight.

You say that you hear us and understand the urgency. But no matter how sad and angry I am, I do not want to believe that. Because if you really understood and continued to not act, then you would be evil. And that I refuse to believe.

If we cannot stay below warming of 1 and ½ degrees, it causes a risk of irreversible chain reactions that will be beyond human control. Those figures do not include tipping points, air pollution, and equity for climate justice. It also assumes that my generation will suck hundreds of billions of tons of carbon out of the air and that technology does not yet exist.

How dare you assume this can be solved with business as usual and some technical solutions. With today's emission levels our entire carbon budget will be gone in 8 and ½ years. There will not be any solutions presented her today because these numbers are too uncomfortable, and you are not mature enough to tell it like it is.

Young people are starting to understand how you are betraying us. The eyes of all future generations are upon you. If you choose to fail us, I say to you, we will never forgive you. We will not let you get away with this. Right here, right now is where we draw the line.

The world is waking up and change is coming whether you like it or not. Thank you.

On Monday night, in response to Thunberg's impassioned speech to the UN, President Trump tweeted sarcastically, "she seems like a very happy young girl looking forward to a bright and wonderful future. So nice to see!" Thunberg promptly edited her Twitter bio to read: "A very happy young girl looking forward to a bright and wonderful future."

6. Greta turns her back on politics for climate change.

Greta Thunberg's rebuke of Congress took showed no favor to heroes of the left who have styled themselves friends of the environment. She characterized partisan efforts that envision an idealized future as unhelpful dreams, and her criticism culminated in these words:

"No matter how political the background to this crisis may be, we must not allow this to continue to be a partisan political question. The climate and ecological crisis is beyond party politics. And our main enemy right now is not our political opponents. Our main enemy now is physics. And we cannot make deals with physics."

The Green New Deal depicts the climate crisis as a liberal cause, which ensures conservative opposition. Greta said the climate crisis is a universal cause. Conservatives need a way to get on board. It's difficult for them to support a policy that evokes the New Deal.

To explain Greta's sudden, global impact, people have begun speaking of her superpowers. One might be that at 16 she understands political reality better than some who have spent their lives in politics. Massachusetts Sen. Edward Markey has been in Congress more than 40 years, often leading the climate charge there. Markey is one of the good guys on climate, by all accounts, one of the best.

He works with a mixture of political fantasy and convenient compromise in his personal life. He rides in a large limousine, not an electric car. Maybe that explains why Markey, hasn't gotten the job done. Here are Greta's words about that.

"Wherever I go I seem to be surrounded by fairytales. Business leaders, elected officials all across the political spectrum spending their time making up and telling bedtime stories that soothe us, that make us go back to sleep. These are 'feel-good' stories about how we are going to fix everything. How wonderful everything is going to be when we have 'solved' everything. But the problem we are facing is not that we lack the ability to dream, or to imagine a better world. The problem now is that we need to wake up. It's time to face the reality, the facts, the science. And the science doesn't mainly speak of 'great opportunities to create the society we always wanted'. It tells of unspoken human sufferings, which will get worse and worse the longer we delay action – unless we start to act now. And yes, of course a sustainable transformed world will include lots of new benefits. But you have to understand. This is not primarily an opportunity to create new green jobs, new businesses or green economic growth. This is above all an emergency, and not just any emergency. This is the biggest crisis humanity has ever faced."

The Republican Party used to support climate action. We owe our participation in the Paris Agreement not just to Barack Obama, who committed us to it, but to George H.W. Bush, who ratified the treaty that created the United Nations Framework on Climate Change.

Before long, Republicans could scarcely admit that science was true without being ousted from office by the Tea Party. And now denialism is personified in the Commander in Chief. So Greta resists the temptation to side with the friendlies. It was Obama who told Greta, over a fistbump last week, "You and me, we're a team." And though Greta went along with that, she didn't change her message. Moments later, speaking to Obama's Capitol Hill allies, including Markey, she said, "I know you're trying, but just not hard enough."

Greta's most important superpower is her integrity. She's not going to take a limo back to the hotel. She's not going to compromise for convenience. She's not going to compromise for feel-good friends or would-be allies. She's going to keep telling the truth. She sailed here just to insist that we read and heed the science. Integrity secures her a place in the history of activism. But she doesn't want our praise. She wants us to take real action. Let's do.

7. Greta interviewed by Amy Goodman for Democracy Today

AMY GOODMAN : So, before you went global — I met you in Poland — before we came, seeing your Twitter feed, it said — at the time, you were 15 — "15-year-old climate activist with Asperger's." That's a part we didn't talk about yet, the Asperger's. When were you diagnosed? And how do you think that contributes to your concern and your singular focus on this issue?

GRETA THUNBERG: When I'm really interested in something, I get superfocused on that. And I can spend hours upon hours not getting tired of reading about it and still be interested to learn more about it. And that is very common for people on the autism spectrum. And yeah, and it just — I think that was one of the reasons why, why I was one of the few who really reacted to the climate crisis, because I couldn't connect the dots why people were just going on like before and still saying, "Yes, climate change is very important." I don't get that double moral, in a way, the difference from between what — between what you know and what you say and what you do, how you act. And for me, it's called cognitive dissonance. And I don't really — I, in a way, I walk the walk. If I decide to do something, then I do it. And so, yeah.

AMY GOODMAN: You have called being on the spectrum your superpower. Why?

GRETA THUNBERG: Because it helps me see things in a way that others might not see, and it just helps me be different, which I think is a superpower in a society where everyone is the same, where everyone thinks the same, everyone looks the same, everyone does the same things. And so I think that is something to really be proud of, that you are different. And in such a crisis like this, we need to think outside the box. We need outside-the-box thinking. We cannot continue thinking like we are today, within our current system. And we need to — and then we need people who think outside the box and who can see this from a different perspective. And, of course, it's not always only a gift and a superpower, that many people suffer from — suffer from it, because they cannot get the right adjustments they need, and they are not living under the right circumstances, which I didn't, as well, for a long time. But now I do. And —

AMY GOODMAN: So, talk about how you've decided to live your life. Yes, you do this climate strike at least once a week, and we'll talk about what you're doing here, as well, in the United States, but the personal decisions you've made that are also political decisions — for example, what you eat, what you wear, how you travel.

GRETA THUNBERG: Yes. I think it was two or three, maybe four years ago, I stopped flying, because that seemed like a big thing to do, because the impact, the climate impact of aviation on a global scale. I mean, individually, it is such a big — it has such a big carbon footprint. And so I just decided I'm not going to fly anymore. And that, of course, was a lot of trouble for my family, because they wanted us to go on vacation and so on. So, I was kind of a troublemaker. But then

I actually convinced them — I guilted them into also doing it, first my mom, and then my dad, as well, and my sister, as well. And then also I am vegan. And I have shop-stop. It means that you don't buy new things, consume new things, unless you absolutely have to. And just these small things I can do in my everyday life, apart from activism and highlighting the problem.

AMY GOODMAN: So, in terms of being a vegan, explain what that means.

GRETA THUNBERG: That I don't use any products made from animals — I mean, any — I don't eat, for example —

AMY GOODMAN: Any animal products?

GRETA THUNBERG: — any animal products. I don't use any animal products, both because of ethical and environmental and climate reasons.

AMY GOODMAN: In terms of clothes, you don't buy new clothes?

GRETA THUNBERG: No. Either I buy second-hand or I receive clothes from someone else, or I just keep my own clothes, maybe use my sister's clothes or my mother's or father's clothes.

AMY GOODMAN: So, when we saw you in Poland at the U.N. climate summit in Katowice, talk about how you got there. If you don't fly, talk about how you get around.

GRETA THUNBERG: I go by bus, by train, electrical car, and sailboat now, as well. And it takes a lot of time. And, of course, I'm not saying that everyone should stop flying and start sailing everywhere. But it was — I thought that I am one of the very few people in the world who can actually do this and who has this opportunity to do this trip. And then I thought, "Why not?" And it sure gained a lot of attention.

AMY GOODMAN: So, I want to go to the speech you gave when we saw you in Poland in Katowice at the U.N. climate summit. This is a clip of what you had to say to the U.N. secretary-general and all those who were gathered for the U.N. climate summit, for the COP.

GRETA THUNBERG: Today we use 100 million barrels of oil every single day. There are no politics to change that. There are no rules to keep that oil in the ground. So we can no longer save the world by playing by the rules, because the rules have to be changed. So we have not come here to beg the world leaders to care for our future. They have ignored us in the past, and they will ignore us again. We have come here to let them know that change is coming, whether they like it or not. The people will rise to the challenge. And since our leaders are behaving like children, we will have to take the responsibility they should have taken long ago. Thank you.

AMY GOODMAN: That's Greta Thunberg, speaking at the U.N. climate summit in Poland when she was 15 years old. As you watch this clip, Greta, you were smiling. Why?

GRETA THUNBERG: It's always fun to see, because it's — I don't know — just the way I talked and the way I — it is a pretty radical thing. It's pretty radical things to say in front of the secretary-general of the U.N. And I remember that speech, because, before, I had prepared a speech, and my father read it through. And he was like, "You cannot say this. This is too radical. And you will embarrass yourself, and you will embarrass everyone, because you cannot say this." And then I just say, "OK." And I — and I cut it out.

AMY GOODMAN: What was it that you were saying?

GRETA THUNBERG: We can no longer save the world by playing by the rules. And, I mean, that's — or if it was the "Why should I be studying for a future that soon may be no more?" and so on. It was something like that. And I cut it out so that he would see it and be calm, because he was very stressed. And then, of course, I memorized that, those sentences, and so I said them anyways during the speech.

G RETA THUNBERG: Deforestation of our great forests, toxic air pollution, loss of insects and wildlife, the acidification of our oceans, these are all disastrous trends, being accelerated by a way of life that we, here in our financially fortunate part of the world, see as our right to simply carry on.

GRETA THUNBERG: And after that, I think I went to Rome. Yeah.

AMY GOODMAN: You mean you went to see the pope?

GRETA THUNBERG: Yeah, to Rome and to the Italian Senate and to see the pope. And yeah. And then to London.

AMY GOODMAN: Let's talk about visiting the pope, what that meant to you, and what the pope has said about the climate crisis, and what you said to him.

GRETA THUNBERG: Yes. I mean, he has been pretty outspoken about this. So I think that it's good that he's talking about this. And he was very supportive. And he said that I should continue doing this. And so, yeah, it was incredible to meet him, of course. And I was very honored to have the chance to do that and to speak to him.

AMY GOODMAN: And when you give these speeches, who do you consult? I mean, when we saw you in Poland, also on the show we had Kevin Anderson, the well-known climate scientist. Frankly, he didn't want to come on with you, because he said, "Give Greta all the time. She's much more important than I am." But you two sat together. Do you speak with climate scientists?

GRETA THUNBERG: I do, very often. I ask them for, like, advice and how should I phrase this and so on, so that there won't be any misunderstandings in what I'm saying, and also to — I mean, they help me a lot to — they read through my speeches to make sure that all the facts are correct. And I can just — if I wonder something, I can just email some of them or text, and then they often reply very, very quickly. So they are very helpful.

AMY GOODMAN: Talk about the issue of climate justice and what that means to you, Greta.

GRETA THUNBERG: Well, I mean, you can explain it in different ways. But an incredibly important thing in that is that those who have caused the climate crisis the most are those who often are going to be the least affected, and the opposite: Those who have caused it, contributed to it the least are most likely the ones to be most affected. And therefore, we must make sure that, of course, that we can help these people and that it is not so unfair in everything.

AMY GOODMAN: So, Greta Thunberg, I want to talk about the movements all over the world, that you are very much a part of and are inspiring. When you went to Britain, you spoke in the British Parliament, but you also spoke at an Extinction Rebellion protest. And we want to play a clip.

GRETA THUNBERG: We are now facing an existential crisis, the climate crisis and ecological crisis, which have never been treated as crisis before. They have been ignored for decades. And for way too long, the politicians and the people in power have gotten away with not doing anything at all to fight the climate crisis and the ecological crisis. But we will make sure that they will not get away with it any longer.

AMY GOODMAN: Greta, there you are, addressing a group at the Extinction Rebellion. That group was just really formulating when we were in Poland. They were there in Britain, starting to superglue themselves to places like ExxonMobil headquarters and other places. Can you talk about the significance of this movement?

GRETA THUNBERG: Yes. I mean, the Extinction Rebellion have really had a massive impact, I think, on our debate, especially in Europe, maybe not as much here, but that they are using civil disobedience, because they are saying, like,

"We won't get your attention otherwise." And that is very effective. And so, it is really incredible to see what they are doing. And it's that, along with Fridays for Future and many other movements, countless of other climate and environmental movements — I think we work together very well. And I think that we, together, have succeeded in making this a priority. It feels like people are slowly starting to wake up a bit more, and it has become more important for people, the climate and ecological crisis. So I think that that is very good. Of course, it's not enough. Of course, it's way too slow. But it's still — it's still something.

AMY GOODMAN: Greta Thunberg, the 16-year-old Swedish climate activist. When we come back, she talks about her two-week journey aboard a zero-emissions sailboat to New York. Stay with us.

[break]

AMY GOODMAN: "Slipping Through My Fingers" by the Swedish group Abba. This is Democracy Now! I'm Amy Goodman, as we return to my interview with Greta Thunberg, the 16-year-old Swedish climate activist who has inspired millions across the globe to demand action to prevent catastrophic climate change. Ahead of the U.N. Climate Action Summit she'll address later this month, Greta arrived in New York after a two-week transatlantic voyage aboard a zero-emissions sailboat. I asked her to describe the journey.

GRETA THUNBERG: I got here on a sailboat, emission-free race sailboat. And it was actually a very good experience. I wish more people had the opportunity to do it, because it was incredible. And you might think that it was scary and hard and rough. But I didn't feel like that at all. I wasn't — I was very lucky. I didn't feel seasick at all during these two weeks. And we went very fast; we hit 30 knots, I think, two times. And that is very fast for a sailing boat.

AMY GOODMAN: And what was it like being out at sea? I mean, this was completely new for you. Describe the experience.

GRETA THUNBERG: Yeah.

AMY GOODMAN: Most people never take a journey like this.

GRETA THUNBERG: Before I went on the sailboat, I didn't really have — I chose to not have any expectations, because I just thought that I — I'll just do it and enjoy it on the way. But it was actually not that bad.

AMY GOODMAN: You never got seasick?

GRETA THUNBERG: No. And it was just amazing to be in this wilderness and to see the wildlife there, with so many dolphins and other wildlife. And if it was calm, then during the nights you could see the stars very clearly, and you can see the Milky Way. And yeah, so it was — it felt very good to be disconnected, to not have contact with people outside, unless through, I mean, satellite phone and so on.

AMY GOODMAN: Your sails, the sails on this boat, these black sails, said, in white letters, "Unite behind the science." Why did you choose that?

GRETA THUNBERG: I chose — I mean, they gave me an opportunity, like, "You can write something on the sail if you want. We are making new sails. And if you want, you can write something on them." And then I thought, "Yeah." And it was — I don't know. I chose it because that is what I want people to do. I want people to unite behind the science, because I am not — all I am telling people to do now is to unite behind the science. And that is what we have to realize, that that is what we have to do right now.

AMY GOODMAN: Let me ask you about a New York Times op-ed piece, a column in The New York Times, that was written by Christopher Caldwell. It's headlined "The Problem with Greta Thunberg's Climate Activism: Her radical approach is at odds with democracy." Caldwell writes, "Normally Ms. Thunberg would be unqualified to debate in a democratic forum." He ends his piece by saying, "Democracy often calls for waiting and seeing. Patience may be democracy's cardinal virtue. Climate change is a serious issue. But to say, 'We can't wait,' is to invite a problem just as grave," he says. Greta Thunberg, if you can respond to Christopher Caldwell.

GRETA THUNBERG: There's nothing I can say to them. Just unite behind the science. I'm not the one who's saying these things. I'm not the one who we should be listening to. And I say that all the time. I say we need to listen to the scientists.

AMY GOODMAN: And he ends by saying we have to wait.

GRETA THUNBERG: Yeah, we have waited 30 years. And I think we have been patient and been waiting and seeing in

30 years. And I think it's time to actually realize the urgency of the problem and to do something.

AMY GOODMAN: It may shock people to hear that you are getting slammed on Twitter — also praised to the heavens by millions of people. But what do you think that means when you get slammed?

GRETA THUNBERG: I mean, you could see it in different ways. Of course, it's sad that people spend their time doing this, when they could be doing something good instead. But you can also see it as something positive, that it means that you have an impact, that these people feel like they feel threatened by you. And that means you have made a difference. And I think this movement has made a difference; otherwise, they wouldn't be spending their time trying to discredit us and to mock us.

AMY GOODMAN: I'd like to talk more about the attack on climate activists. I want to turn the U.N. high commissioner for human rights, Michelle Bachelet, the former president of Chile, talking about the attacks on climate activists, including you.

MICHELLE BACHELET: The office and special rapporteurs have noted attacks on environmental human rights defenders in virtually every region, particularly in Latin America. I am disheartened by this violence, and also by the verbal attacks on young activists, such as Greta Thunberg and others, who galvanize support for prevention of the harm their generation may bear. The demands made by environmental defenders and activists are compelling, and we should respect, protect and fulfill their rights.

AMY GOODMAN: So that's Michelle Bachelet, now the U.N. high commissioner for human rights. She was the president of Chile, which will be hosting the U.N. climate summit, the COP25, in December, where Greta will be. It was going to be Brazil, but they withdrew their invitation to host the COP, because of the far-right climate change-denying President Jair Bolsonaro. Greta, if you can talk about what Michelle Bachelet said? She singled you out, talking about climate activists and attacks on them, but so many climate activists feel under siege. And also talk about your plans leading up to COP25, the U.N. summit, as you make your way through the Americas.

GRETA THUNBERG: Yes. Many climate and environmental activists are being attacked, and they are being, in some cases, even killed. And so I'm not the one who we should be focusing on in these cases. And it's just horrible that you are trying to stand up for something that should be taken for granted — a living world and a functioning climate — and it's just unbelievable to see what some people have to go through. And, of course, I know many, many activists, young activists especially, that are being attacked on the internet and are being lied about and being mocked, sometimes by elected officials and by respected journalists. And I don't understand how you can attack someone like that.

And, I mean, sometimes these activists get — they get sad because of it. And that, of course, impacts them in a way that they feel like they cannot continue. And that is, of course, what they want; that is the goal of these attacks. So, I just, and the other activists who support, we support each other. We just have to comfort each other and to be there for each other and to say, like, "Don't care about these people, because all they are doing is to — their goal is to waste your time and to make you tired of this and to make you want to stop, because what you are doing is actually good."

AMY GOODMAN: You just recently tweeted that Amazon workers, 900 of them, based in Seattle — it's the first time ever — they're going to also strike on September 20th.

GRETA THUNBERG: Yeah.

AMY GOODMAN: What does that mean to you?

GRETA THUNBERG: To me and to the movement, it means incredibly much, because we have lots of unions who are planning to strike, so, I mean, adults striking from their work. And that is so incredibly important to show that this is such an — this is not just for children or teenagers. This is for everyone. And what we are doing, we are not, of course — I mean, we are striking to disrupt the system, to create attention. And I just hope that it will turn out well.

AMY GOODMAN: So let's talk about what you're doing in these coming days. You're heading down to Washington, D.C., the nation's capital. On Friday, what are your plans? That's Friday, September 13th.

GRETA THUNBERG: Yes. On Friday, I am going to — this Friday the 13th, I am going to join the school strike for the climate outside the White House in Washington, D.C. And I —

AMY GOODMAN: Do you protest every single week on Fridays?

GRETA THUNBERG: Yes.

AMY GOODMAN: Wherever you are in the world?

GRETA THUNBERG: Yes, even on the boat. Every week, no matter where I am, on Fridays, I will protest and demonstrate for the climate, outside the parliament or local government building or town hall or anything.

AMY GOODMAN: So, on the 13th, you're doing it in front of the White House.

GRETA THUNBERG: Yes.

AMY GOODMAN: When you landed last week, you landed on Wednesday evening. Friday, you were in front of the United Nations.

GRETA THUNBERG: Yeah.

AMY GOODMAN: With those who you inspired, who had been protesting in front of the United Nations for many weeks, almost a year. So then talk about the following week, September 20th, what your plans are and what people's plans are around the globe.

GRETA THUNBERG: Yes. On the 20th, we are planning a new global strike. And we call for people of all ages to join us, not just children. Adults are, of course, welcome, as well, to strike from their work. And so, I will be in New York the 20th of

September to join the strike here. And then, on the 27th, there is also a global strike.

AMY GOODMAN: And then you head, eventually, in December, to the U.N. climate summit in Chile. Talk about the journey you plan to take between September and December.

GRETA THUNBERG: Yes. In December, I am planning to go to the COP25, and which is in Santiago. So, it's quite a long way there from here, so I will have to make sure to leave on time and travel through the North and South American continent, and probably sail for a bit where it's too hard to travel. And then I will be there. And I don't know exactly what I will be doing there, but I have been invited to speak there. And then, after that, we'll see what I'm doing.

AMY GOODMAN: And finally, your message to young people, people perhaps who don't vote — that's true — but are finding their place in the world? What do you say to them? And you can look directly into the camera.

GRETA THUNBERG: My message to the young people of the world is that right now we are facing an existential crisis, I mean, the climate and ecological crisis, and it will have a massive impact on our lives in the future, but also now, especially in vulnerable communities. And I think that we should wake up, and we should also try to wake the adults up, because they are the ones who — their generation is the ones who are mostly responsible for this crisis, and we need to hold them accountable. We need to hold the people in power accountable for what they have been doing to us and future generations and other living species on Earth. And we need to get angry and understand what is at stake. And then we need to transform that anger into action and to stand together united and just never give up.

AMY GOODMAN: That's 16-year-old Swedish climate activist Greta Thunberg in her first extended broadcast interview here in the United States. She'll be protesting in front to the White House on Friday, then taking part in the global climate strike on Friday, September 20th, here in New York. On Monday, September 23rd, she'll address the U.N. General Assembly at the U.N. Climate Action Summit. And she'll be at the U.N. climate summit in Santiago, Chile, in December. Democracy Now! will be there, as well, covering all of these events. Greta Thunberg on Democracy Now with Amy Goodman.

8. Two more interviews with Trevor Noah and Acie Cargill

Greta on Daily Show with Trevor Noah

T   You are not just affecting young people. In Europe at least there is the Greta effect and more people are taking trains instead of flying. In general there is much more interest in younger people about the climate change. Why do you think that is?

G   I think it is because younger people feel it is more of a direct threat. A lot of older people think "Oh, I won't be alive then anyway." But everyone must realize there are consequences that everyone will feel and they are happening now.

T   What do you think is he most important part of climate change that people don't understand?

G   Everything. There seems to be a general lack of understanding and so naturally most people just don't seem to care about the climate. 200 species go extinct every day and people just don't notice. So they don't really care. We have less than 8 and ½ years until we have completely used up our carbon budget and then there will be no chance of making lasting effects for the better.

T   What do you think people should do and what should the government be doing?

G I would like people to become informed about the science and try to understand it and maybe push the leaders to try to fix it

T Do you notice a difference in the way people discuss the Climate Crisis from Sweden to America?

G Yes. Here people discuss it as something they believe in or don't believe in. Where I come from people accept it as a fact.

T New York City is an assault on the senses. What has stuck out the most on New York City

G Yes, just everything. It is so loud. People talk so loud. What I first noticed as we arrived in New York Harbor was the smell. Of course, it is pollution. It is indescribable coming from the ocean to New York City.

T That is a perfect description of New York City. It is indescribable and it smells.

Greta interviewed by Acie Cargill

A By the way, we are both vegans and we both wear second hand clothes, we love love animals, neither of us fly in planes. We both try to to do what we can to influence others to be better people and citizens of the earth.

G Well I am happy to meet you. I have read the booklets you wrote about me.

A   Today is your Friday school strike to be held in front of the White House in Washington DC. I'm glad you are getting around and getting more exposure for fighting climate change

G   Yes. And next Friday I will be back in new York and the following Friday school strike will be in Montreal in Canada. That will be September 27

A   I think you will find the Canadians to be more conducive to your words and your ideas.

G   yes. I am hoping I get to meet Mr. Trudeau

A   There are some leaders in the world who are accepting of human rights and he seems to be one of them. What do you expect to be the reaction from the White House today?

G   I don't expect any reaction or even a recognition of our student strike. I hope I am wrong, but it seems like the American President will just ignore our presence on his front walk.

A   It would be wonderful if you can influence him to at least consider the problems and maybe change his attitude even a little bit. If he changes his attitude then there are 100 million people who will change their attitudes also.

G   That is the first step. It is what we want. For people to consider the science of climate and start thinking about it.

A   It is such a big subject. Overwhelming to the average person who looks into the sky and it seems no different than they can ever remember.

G   But it is different. The greenhouse gases might be invisible to the naked eye, but they are there and they are causing global warming. You can tell by all the ice melting in the Arctic and Antarctica and even in highland glaciers.

A   I have read about Island nations in the Pacific watching the sea level rise little by little and finally may inundate their homes.

G   The climate of the Earth is so finely tuned. There are already terrible fires and flooding and storms like the increase in hurricanes. And they are stronger.

A   I see you have been invited to speak at Congressional hearings. At least by the democrats. I don't understand why there should be difference in attitude by the political parties. The earth is in crisis and should be dealt with by all people in power.

G   Including the President. When he sees the millions of students demonstrating their displeasure with being ignored by the leaders of this country, I would think he would at least have a meeting with some of us. Maybe even me.

A   And what will you say to the president? Pretend I am him. What will you say?

G   Mr. President. I respect the hard work you have done to become president of this great country. Will you give the science of the environment a chance to convince you that we have big problems, but they are not yet insurmountable. Please recognize that the United States, and of course, China, are the biggest contributors to the climate problems. Please start thinking about it at least and consider the benefits to the entire world and the future of humanity and all life on this planet.

A   Well, that statement makes a lot of sense. I hope you will be able to open his mind to the possibilities of the climate crisis and what can be done. He is a smart man. He just has to start thinking about it. You can do it, Greta.

G   Thank you, Acie. I think you are right. I sure will try to do whatever I can if the President will give me a chance to speak to him.

9. Who is Greta Thunberg by Max Bolyn

Her speeches are calls to action. One of her most widely cited quotes is that, "I don't want you to be hopeful. I want you to panic. I want you to feel the fear I feel every day. And then I want you to act. I want you to act as you would in a crisis. I want you to act as if the house was on fire—because it is." She has also cited a number of the recent findings by the Intergovernmental Panel on Climate Change (IPCC), backing up her call for urgent action.

Looking at my Twitter feed, there are many reactions by reporters, a bunch of economists and other social scientists belittling her efforts. The arguments usually go something like this:

"Kids should stay in school and learn and then when they are well educated effect change". Awesome. We and the generations prior to us did that and have you looked at the state of the world around us?

She is creating an unjustified degree of panic. The house is not on fire. We have plenty of time to fix the climate change problem. Read an IPCC report or two. If you don't like reading on a screen, I'll send you a signed paper copy. We do not have much time left to act.

She claims that we know what it takes to fix the problem. Well, we sort of do. Some mix of carbon pricing and technological and possibly input standards will do the trick, or at least get us well on our way.

Finally, they say that there may be a media firm or a green technology firm behind her campaign. Well, that is just outrageous! Fossil fuel companies don't do that at all, right? They do not hire lobbyists, advertising firms and plain old bribes to get their way! Come on. Let's not be ridiculous. Should we require that all kid activists fund their campaigns from money they earn from their lemonade stands, while fossil fuel companies get to employ their generous government sponsored subsidies and tax break money?

Moral suasion is essentially what your grandparents have taught you and is often called "doing the right thing". Ms. Thunberg is making a strong case in support of the point that we are failing her and future generations and that this is not consistent with the values we, supposedly, have regardless of faith. She reminds us of this very effectively and politicians across the world have taken notice.

Greta Thunberg may well be an important focal point in the problem of solving the climate dilemma. When people are asked about the issues that concern them, the environment often comes out at the very end of a top ten list.

Her visibility achieves two things in my view. First, it draws attention to the climate problem, as the media campaign she has started is first rate. Second, solving the climate problem has suffered historically from a lack of coordination as countries have had a really hard time agreeing on what we will really do to address this challenge. Rallying behind Ms.

Thunberg's call for action at the UN in a few weeks may just do the trick – especially if the youth of the world are behind her. She has never claimed to be a climate scientist or economist. She is standing on top of a very large mountain of science and telling us to pay attention to this issue.

10. Closing comments

In a column on Al-Jazeera English, writer Andrew Mitrovica came to the defense of Thunberg as he referred to those attacking her as "scientifically illiterate bullies." According to Mitrovica, it is Thunberg's attributes—including her fearlessness and ability to speak and act so matter-of-factly—that makes hers such a potent voice. He writes:

"She disdains celebrity. She makes no claim to heroism. She rebuffs efforts to idolize her. She isn't calculating or preoccupied with fame or ego. There is nothing false about her. She speaks plainly, without affectation or embroidery.

In words and deeds, Thunberg is the embodiment of philosopher Howard Zinn's admonition: "We don't have to engage in grand, heroic actions to participate in the process of change. Small acts, when multiplied by millions of people, can quietly become a power no government can suppress, a power that can transform the world."

Greta comments on NPR:

When haters go after your looks and differences, it means they have nowhere left to go. And then you know you're winning! I have Aspergers and that means I'm sometimes a bit different from the norm. And—given the right circumstances—being different is a superpower".

I was about ten years old and my teacher told me about climate Change and global warming and caused by humans and I thought that sounded very strange because if it were true that we are causing the problem that it should be our first priority and we won't be thinking of anything else. But it is not their top priority and I am the kind of person that doesn't like when people say one thing and do another thing. And that's the case with climate change. Everyone says it is very important yet they carry on as before. And I started reading about it and the more I read about, the more I understood. Once you understand about the climate crisis you cannot not understand. You will always be thinking about it.

She said she has nothing to say to people who refuse to believe in the scientific warnings about the climate crisis. The leaders owe it to the young people to give them hope. But I don't want their hope. I want them to feel panic, the way I feel panic every day. So they will act. Act the way they should in a crisis. I want them to act as if their house is on fire. Because it is.

www.ingramcontent.com/pod-product-compliance
Lightning Source LLC
Chambersburg PA
CBHW061528250726
48657CB00005B/2131